Old EAST LOTHIAN VILLAGES

by
David Anderson

These children are at the door of their home at Burnfoot, near Stenton. The house belonged to Beil Estate and the children's father was employed on the estate lands. Cottages such as this were old-fashioned relics of an earlier time and would once have been thatched, with one end used as a byre while the family lived in the other end. In the nineteenth century many such cottages were improved or replaced by landowners and farmers. The children in the picture most probably went to school at Stenton, but it is likely that they regularly started at new schools as East Lothian's valuation rolls show a rapid turnover of residents here. This pattern was found because agricultural workers might change employers as frequently as once a year and their families got used to moving from one tied cottage to another.

ACKNOWLEDGEMENTS

Most of the pictures come from the author's own collection but those on the front cover, inside front cover, back cover, and pages 2, 21, 22, 23 (lower), 26 and 41 appear by courtesy of East Lothian Council Library Service and their Local History Centre collections, for which thanks are extended.

FURTHER READING

Such is the interest in local history that several accounts of individual villages featured in this book have been published in recent years, and the *Transactions* of the East Lothian Antiquarian and Field Naturalists Society include many authoritative accounts on specific matters of East Lothian interest. For readers seeking a more detailed account of old East Lothian, the Library Service have recently republished in one volume *Reminiscences and Notices of the Parishes of East Lothian* by John Martine. Originally published in the late nineteenth century, Martine covers many entertaining personalities and events, providing a wealth of detail about our old East Lothian villages. (Please note that none of these publications are available from Stenlake Publishing.)

Harvest was the busiest time of the rural year, but the other seasons had their own demands. Before the near universal application of herbicides to arable crops, most farms employed gangs of labourers, many of them women, to weed and hoe growing crops. The women fieldworkers of East Lothian had their own distinctive headgear, known as an 'ugli', which they wore to protect them from the sun, wind and rain. It was essentially a cotton bonnet stiffened at the front into a high peak or hood with wicker boning so that it could be pushed forward or back as circumstances demanded. Several members of this group are wearing uglis.

INTRODUCTION

This book looks at some of the villages scattered throughout the rural landscape of the county of East Lothian. The district became substantially larger during administrative reforms in the 1970s and the redrawn boundaries incorporated large parts of the old county of Midlothian on the west. As these changes happened in the recent past, well after the images included in this book were recorded, it seemed appropriate to simply consider those villages and parishes that were part of the historic county.

For most of its history, the boundaries of East Lothian essentially conformed to natural features provided by nature and formed a territory that was roughly diamond shaped. On the territory's two landward sides there are the uplands of the Lammermuirs; the Firth of Forth and the North Sea together form the other two sides. Between these limits is a relatively level plain that falls gently to the sea. The plain is dotted with a few scattered hilly outcrops and cut across the middle by the valley of the River Tyne – the only significant watercourse. The soil on the plain has been improved over the centuries but has long been reckoned rich: it has always played an important role in feeding Scotland. In fact, strategic control of East Lothian has often been a prerequisite for successful command of the whole country. Some of the best farmland lies on the west and is underlain by a number of shallow coal seams; both resources have played their role in supplying nearby Edinburgh, but also enabled early industrialisation in the Tranent-Prestonpans area. By contrast, the rest of the county has remained predominantly agricultural in outlook. Barley and wheat both grow well over the entire county. In the eastern districts potatoes, carrots and root crops were grown on a large scale; in the western parts market gardens supplied fruit and a wide range of vegetables. On the higher ground stock rearing was and is still a major activity.

The land of East Lothian begins to appear in the written historical record during the Roman Period (although archaeological discoveries show that it has been settled for thousands of years). The local British tribes (the Votadini or later the Gododdin) appear to have come to an 'accommodation' or settlement with the Romans, perhaps acting as a buffer state to the north of Hadrian's Wall. One of their centres has been identified on the summit of Traprain Law in the centre of East Lothian (one of Scotland's earliest known town settlements). Dunbar, Garvald, Tranent and Aberlady are examples of settlement names with roots in this period; the Peffer Burn, Doon Hill and many other landscape features contain name elements from the same time.

There was a brief flowering of the native British culture as regional kingdoms asserted their independence and strong leaders carved out territories to support their warbands after the Romans left Britain. Very few certain facts are known from this period, but some have been separated from fancy by comparing surviving myths and legends from many sources. As an example, the name Lothian is supposed to derive from King Lot of the Gododdin who may have been the grandfather of St Kentigern. (Although Kentigern – or Mungo as he is otherwise known – eventually settled at Glasgow, his mother was an exiled princess from Traprain.) Christianity was certainly an early feature of society in East Lothian – most of what we know of this period comes from written accounts of early saints: hagiographies documenting events and miracles in their lives.

The kingdom of the Gododdin is believed to have fallen to an invading power in the seventh century. English-speaking conquerors swept up from Northumbria and incorporated the whole of Lothian as the northernmost province of their kingdom. Theirs is a very obvious legacy in today's place names: Whittinghame, Tyninghame, Oldhamstocks and Innerwick all preserve evidence of Northumbrian settlement. Archaeologically, excellent evidence of the invaders has been found at Doon Hill and Dunbar and the written record begins to fill out with more names of people and accounts of significant events. Strategically, possession of the Lothians brought the Northumbrians into direct contact with the Scots and Picts of the north and the Strathclyde Britons of the west. Several centuries of interaction left their mark, but by the eleventh century Lothian was firmly incorporated into the kingdom of the Scots.

One of the reasons why Scotland gained Lothian was that the Northumbrians were under pressure from the southern Viking kingdom established at York (Viking bands also ravaged the East Lothian coastline and sacked the church of Tyninghame). Despite fighting back against the Scots, the Northumbrians were never able to regain control of the lands between Tweed and Forth and eventually appear to have settled for negotiated boundaries secured on dynastic marriages between each royal house. The offspring of one of these marriages, Gospatrick, self-styled 'King of Cumbria' and for a brief period Earl of Northumbria, founded a dynasty that controlled much of East Lothian until the fifteenth century. His descendants were the Earls of Dunbar and March: the parishes of Whittinghame, Stenton, Prestonkirk, Spott, Dunbar, Innerwick and Oldhamstocks and many other places nearby were controlled and shaped by the earls and their adherents. The remains of their fortresses are still a significant element in the landscape.

In the early medieval period East Lothian was gradually divided into the ecclesiastical parishes that survive today. In a parallel and complementary process the land itself was parcelled into estates that pertained to the Crown, the Church or to magnates such as the Dunbars. Several large expanses of common land were also parts of the burghs of Dunbar and Haddington: while Dunbar Common in the Lammermuirs has remained virtually deserted, Haddington's common of Gladsmuir became a parish in its own right. Most of the large estates were controlled from a castle or tower and new settlements grew nearby, secure in their protection (Dirleton is a good example). The territorial subdivisions created a patchwork pattern of communities great and small and although there was succession in land-owning families, where some disappeared and others rose to take their place, the boundaries of the parishes, estates, towns and villages remained essentially unchanged into the twentieth century.

Most of the county's people thus lived in compact territories, places whose existence revolved around the farming year, the offshore fisheries or the collieries to the west. Their settlements continued to grow in number as times became more settled. More land was brought under the plough, but the relative importance of places often altered: examples are the growth of Stenton at the expense of Pitcox, and the near loss of Gullane to enveloping dunes with the corresponding rise of nearby Dirleton. Gradually, the county took on its present form: each farm toun (hamlet) looked to a nearby village for services and supplies beyond its own capacity; in turn the villages looked to the nearest town.

In the eighteenth and early nineteenth centuries a wave of innovation in farming practice created much of today's network of enclosed fields and distinctive farm steadings, often replacing open land worked in partnership by several families based at a farm toun. This process was captured in mid-transition on Forrest's map of the county published in 1799. Other pioneering landowners used their estates for experiments in social engineering, creating model communities like Ormiston and Tyninghame. Some of the tree cover began to be restored to the lowland areas, from where it had been long cleared, creating areas such as Binning Wood and other forests that are still being cropped for timber today.

A century ago, when the earliest pictures in this book were taken, fully half of East Lothian's people lived in a landscape that was still predominantly agricultural. The historic richness of the land was reflected in the presence of many mansions, often incorporating or built alongside towers or castles, left to moulder away as relics of bygone times. Most of the villages had several shops and a good range of craftsmen. They almost always had a school and, if the centre of a parish, one or more churches. Many of the villages were burghs of barony, an old Scottish classification ratified by a feudal charter that specified, usually, rights to a market or fair and varying kinds of rights for the inhabitants. The distinction between this form of burgh and those described as 'royal' centred on autonomy: royal burghs were self-governing whereas burghs of barony pertained to a landowner, usually an aristocrat, and were administered by his appointees. Only a few villages (Gifford was one) had input from the inhabitants in their governance and this was one of the reasons that some of the larger ones were granted autonomy and their own councils in the nineteenth century.

Before the reforms of the 1970s there were seven substantial towns (at least, substantial in East Lothian terms) that had attained self-governing status in the old county. These comprised the three ancient Royal Burghs – Haddington, Dunbar and North Berwick – all of which gained their status in medieval times, and four nineteenth century burghs: Tranent, Prestonpans, East Linton, and the united burgh of Cockenzie and Port Seton. The latter were all 'police burghs', so-called after the Act of Parliament that enabled their establishment. They were granted self-governing status to correct anomalies that had appeared as they grew in population and economic importance.

Images of the towns have been excluded from this book as their burgh status takes them out the 'village' category for present purposes. However, the united settlement of Cockenzie and Port Seton has been included as a special case despite it being a burgh: at heart it is still centred on its harbours and retains its village character. The selection of images is by no means comprehensive: there are simply so many places that might be included. However, it does include places from the east and west as well as from the hills and the coast.

Recent tourism initiatives have promoted a number of self-guiding trails or routes through the hillfoots and along the coast, so that has been the method used to select the order of presentation. The images start with places on the east and progress west via some of the villages of the inland parts of the county, returning along to coast from west to east in the second half of the book.

The School House, Oldhamstocks   No. 3503

Oldhamstocks village green was once its marketplace; the market cross is a sign that the village had a right to hold public fairs and a weekly market. The present cross is a composite, rebuilt on a new site and retaining some original parts that had been found simply lying in gardens nearby. The school in the background was never large, and for a long time the schoolmaster could augment his regular salary by charging a guinea a head for special courses in subjects like navigation and bookkeeping. When the school closed, children in the village had to go to Innerwick, the nearest village to the west. Events like school closures are keenly felt by village communities and it has been a feature of the twentieth century that closures perpetuate declining populations when families with children are prompted to move to avoid inconvenient journeys.

Oldhamstocks is a linear village, a single row of cottages and houses running along the sunny side of a valley on the edge of the Lammermuir. It is well hidden by the hills and lies in the centre of its parish surrounded by farms. Of the latter, those nearer the sea are mostly arable, while those on the inland side concentrate on stock-rearing. The village was the traditional market centre for these farms, with a couple of inns (one claiming Oliver Cromwell as a one-time visitor). The village had a good selection of tradesmen such as a blacksmith, tailor, and shoemaker, and shops including a bakers, grocers and butchers. Now only the combined post office and general store is open. Many of the buildings in the village are listed, as is the eighteenth century wellhead that once provided it with water.

Innerwick is built along two adjacent ridges and its name, meaning the 'Inward Hamlet', derives from Anglian settlers of the first millennium. Later the village and the land nearby were granted by the Crown to a branch of the Stewarts; afterwards it passed to a branch of the Hamilton family. For most of the nineteenth century Innerwick was a prosperous place because of the richness of the fifteen farms surrounding it, many of which were in the hands of improving tenants. When this Edwardian photograph was taken Mrs Hamilton-Nisbet of Biel owned many of these farms and the Hunters of Thurston were in possession of the next largest group. The farmers had plenty of sea-ware (seaweed) available for fertiliser. Local outcrops of limestone were burnt for lime, which was used for dressing the fields. It was farm tenants such as the Lees of Skateraw and Dryburnford who were responsible for taking up the cultivation of turnips, which revolutionised animal husbandry by providing a reliable source of winter feed for farmers on the pastoral lands further inland.

507 Thurston House, Innerwick.

Thurston Manor was designed by John Kinross and was a late addition to the East Lothian landscape when it was built in the nineteenth century. It was demolished in 1952 and an upmarket holiday village and caravan park now occupies the site. Thurston was once the home of the Hunter family and the centre of an impressive estate of farms in Innerwick and Oldhamstocks parishes. Near the house was a stand of fine old trees, while other areas of the estate were also productive woods. Despite its richness as farmland, forestry has always been significant in this district. Many local names suggest the woods have been important for a long time: Woodley, Braidwood, Woodhall and Wadalee are all nearby.

Spott House stands on a crag above a fork in the Spott Burn as it passes through a narrow chasm. The strength of the position is disguised on the west side, as the gorge is covered by a culvert which provides an approach to the building, but this view from the east shows that access to the rear is via a bridge. The house was extensively remodelled in the Scots Baronial style in 1830 by the architect William Burn, but the core is an early defensive tower with many later seventeenth century features. In the thirteenth century much of Spott parish was a territory that formed part of the Earldom of Dunbar. Some of the lands nearby were in the possession of the Knights Templar (the knights of St John), remembered in St John's Well behind the village.

Spott is another linear village, lying on both sides of a single street. It was once busy with the day-to-day life centred around its school, tradesmen, blacksmith and few shops but is a very quiet, pleasant place today. Coming from the Dunbar road its cottages appear one by one as the road curves steeply upward. The first part of the village, called Canon's Row, connects the present with medieval times; the land supported a canon of the collegiate church of Dunbar and the chapel of Spott was his prebend (that is, the canon received the revenue from the church and paid a vicar to conduct services for the villagers).

Although Spott is a peaceful place today, it has had its dark times. Twice, the remnants of Scottish armies have fled through the village from nearby defeats and an old record remarks that once 'many witches were burnt at the head of Spott Loan'. Furthermore, one of the village's ministers was hanged at Edinburgh. Around 1570 the Reverend John Kello, having murdered his wife on a Sunday, preached a stormer of a sermon to his congregation and brazened out the discovery of his wife's body afterwards. Initially it appeared that he might get away with his deed, although he was plagued by dreams and turned to his colleague from Dunbar who drew out the story and alerted the authorities. Kello made a full confession and was duly executed.

Spott Pond was created as a reservoir to maintain the supply of water that Dunbar Town Council had negotiated with local landowners. Once a year, as was their right, the provost, magistrates and council of the nearby town assembled at the pond for their annual fishing trip, a perk that they had secured along with the water rights. This was an occasion when the quality of the picnic was possibly more important than the quantity of the fishing. It is recorded that the leaders of Dunbar frequently returned home 'well refreshed' from their jolly day in the country.

This set of photographs (above and opposite) documents the building of a water filtration plant just outside Spott. Water had been supplied to Dunbar from springs in the neighbourhood when the first wooden pipes were laid in the eighteenth century. Nineteenth century developments saw the building of a compensation pond to provide an even flow for a vastly increased supply. The filtration works ensured the supply met twentieth century requirements, but even this was eventually made redundant when the water supply for the whole of East Lothian was linked together. A network was created with pumping stations to move the supply from the Hopes and Whiteadder reservoirs to the point of use – the domestic tap. However, water from the Lammermuir springs is still being drunk in the twenty-first century, as several bottling operations sell it as natural spring water.

This picture shows the village green at Stenton, another settlement with an Anglian name. The original centre of the parish was a mile or so away at Pitcox – a name generally believed to have Pictish roots, and evidence of another race involved in territorial squabbles in this area during the first millennium. (Pitcox is now just a farm and there is no trace of the medieval settlement.) The round plinth near the middle of the photograph is the base of a tron, or public weighing machine, which has now been partially restored. The tron was used to weigh wool and fleeces brought down from the hills for sale to merchants attending fairs and markets on the green. Most of the buildings in Stenton are built of local red sandstone, including the remains of the old church in the background. The surviving old church tower was used as a doocot after the new church was built and the interior of the old church was used for burials, mostly those of the Hamiltons of Beil who owned much of the parish.

Stenton has a good example of a rural Victorian school. It was built by the County School Board in 1878 behind a triangular green at the west end of the village, near the school it replaced. It is still open and currently increasing its roll. The school was designed to be served by two or three teachers, each looking after composite classes and aided by visiting specialists; for a period only one permanent staff member was necessary. Despite its small size it has separate boys' and girls' entrances on either side of the building. Most pupils leaving the school go on to Dunbar Grammar, although some now travel as far afield as Edinburgh.

Stenton's layout is medieval in origin. The church stands near one end of the village and the old schoolhouse (on the right of this picture) is at the other. Most of the buildings that line the street are now houses, but some were shops and workplaces once. Behind each property and running back from the street was a garden that terminated at the edge of the surrounding fields; these were once used to supply much of the villagers' vegetables. Stenton shares many of the features of nearby burghs and towns, which originated on a similar scale and pattern. The difference is that the towns have continued to grow and develop whereas Stenton remained small-scale; lying away from the major land and sea routes of southern Scotland and of no strategic importance, there was no reason for it to develop further.

Garvald is hidden in a fold of the rising Lammermuir Hills and survived Anglian times with its British name intact (it means 'Rough Burn'). Perhaps it was too out of the way to attract a new overlord in the seventh century invasions. The village is essentially another single street, with the church at one end. This photograph illustrates the general layout from the Lammermuir side. Each of the eclectic mixture of buildings has a garden plot: for much of Garvald's history its tradesmen and shopkeepers were also 'cottars', who provided much of their own provisions from their and their families' labour in their gardens.

GARVALD FROM SOUTH.

92189 J.Y.

At the east end of Garvald the village street takes a sharp turn; a dog-leg leads on to the parish church but at the same place another road runs straight on across a bridge over the Papana Water before winding its way up into the hills; it was once used as a trading route into the borders and was popular with packmen who moved from place to place with their goods. This picture again illustrates the mixture of housing in the village. The large dwellings in the centre are flanked by single-storey cottages; those in the foreground are particularly tiny, but not untypical of early nineteenth century labourers' houses.

William Ferguson was licensed to sell wines and spirits as well as being a general merchant in Garvald during the Edwardian period. From the evidence of this picture, he employed at least three shopmen; the presence of the cart suggests that his customers also received deliveries from the shop. This postcard was used for advertising purposes and for shop business: in this case the card was sent to a wholesaler in Market Street, Edinburgh requesting '5 Bags Good Carrots' to be dispatched by train to Gifford Station 'at once'. Mr Ferguson could reasonably expect to get his carrots the same day. The background of the image shows the mixture of single and two-storey buildings that give Garvald a pleasing look. Many of the older properties are built of a deep-red coloured local sandstone and are roofed with terracotta pantiles.

'Nunraw' means the nuns' row or hamlet. Nunraw House was once owned by the convent of Haddington, but in the sixteenth century passed to a branch of the Hepburns through family interest. (All across East Lothian at that time eager families were competing to acquire former church lands as the impact of the Reformation released substantial estates.) The Hepburns' sixteenth century tower house forms the core of the present Victorian Baronial mansion, which was the result of work by the architect Robert Hay in 1860–1864. The building also incorporates work from other centuries and is complemented by fine ancillary farm buildings and offices.

339 Main Street, Gifford

Gifford is the largest of East Lothian's hill-parish villages. The name derives from the Norman family of Gifford who gained the Barony of Yester from King David I. At that time the village was called Bothans after an early saint venerated at several nearby places (the surrounding ecclesiastical parish was called Yester, from the old British Ystrad, meaning 'valley'). In those days the village lay close to where the Giffords built their castle, now the location of Yester House. The proprietorship of the lands subsequently passed to the Hay family, and when they felt they needed a new mansion and park in the seventeenth century, the villagers were moved to a new planned settlement (with the new name) on the opposite side of the Gifford Water. This view looks up the main street to the parish church. In the foreground is a public well and behind that the village's market cross, built in 1780 in the form of a pillar topped with a heraldic embellishment.

Gifford from Village Green

Gifford village green was once a bleaching field. Handloom weaving was an important trade in many rural villages and East Lothian was once at the forefront of developments in the linen processing industry. The village also boasts two fine inns, one of which, the Tweeddale Arms, is on the right of this picture. These were traditionally at their busiest in March, June and October at the times of the Gifford fairs. Although the fairs were important for sheep, cattle and horse sales, they drew people from miles around for the associated attractions. There were showmen and their rides, coopers and bicker makers, tinsmiths and tinkers, horners and Gypsy horse-traders, and stalls and tradesmen selling all manner of sweets. (Bicker makers made all manner of wooden vessels; horners made vessels and domestic utensils from animal horn.)

The weir in the foreground of this picture of the Gifford Water recalls the time when there were several mills in the village, including a woollen or 'wauk' mill and a meal mill. In the first half of the nineteenth century the country roads and bridges of East Lothian were improved by the application of funds raised by levying tolls on users. The cash was administered by Turnpike Trusts (consisting mainly of local landowners) and the result was well-maintained bridges like this one, many of which are still in use. So too is much of the network of roads that interconnect villages, hamlets, farms and country houses and link them to the main towns of the county.

Glenkinchie Pencaitland.

Photo by
Charles Bruce
Haddington.

Pencaitland is still dominated by Glenkinchie Distillery, the last survivor of the whisky industry in East Lothian and one of very few lowland distilleries in Scotland. In the eighteenth and nineteenth centuries distilleries were widespread and along with their associated maltings and cooperages employed a fair number of hands across the county. There was a ready supply of local grain, good water, and a well-developed infrastructure to tranship the product to market via Dunbar harbour in the east or to Edinburgh and Leith via the roads to the west. Glenkinchie is now a tourist attraction where visitors on guided tours can view all of the stages of whisky production and have an opportunity to sample the local product.

The present layout of the centre and oldest part of Ormiston was the brainchild of John Cockburn, whose family owned most of the nearby land. In the middle of the eighteenth century he began by improving his estates and encouraged his tenants to do the same. Later he decided that a model community would be a much better advertisement for his innovations and employed an English surveyor to lay out new plots. Cockburn built on some of these plots himself but others were feued off (leased) to tenants under the conditions that dwellings should be built at least two storeys high and be of high quality with mortared stone walls and slate roofs. Within a few years many other local proprietors had followed his example, and planned villages became all the rage. They form a continuing feature of the East Lothian landscape today.

Ormiston lies above several productive coal seams that have been worked for centuries. At first the workings were simply shallow pits on a small scale working coal that lay near to the surface, but later the colliers went deeper both from necessity (to win untouched reserves) but also because improvements in technology made this possible. In the nineteenth century an influx of people (many migrating from other Scottish coalfields) found employment in expanding local collieries and Ormiston grew accordingly. The Miners' Institute in this picture was opened in 1925. It provided a centre for the miners, with reading and committee rooms, and a program of activities that included both social events and training courses.

The number of people employed on the land declined throughout the twentieth century, but there were some operations that needed a lot of temporary staff. Work-gangs from the villages and towns were employed at harvest time, especially for lifting potatoes and (as seen here) picking soft fruit. Gangs like this were regularly employed on market farms, of which there were many in the west of the county; good communications installed for the coal industry could be used to get the perishable crops to markets in Edinburgh. The work was demanding and intensive, often going on for as long as there was light. Tallying (weighing and counting up) was done in the field and pickers were paid for the quantity they had collected.

Cockenzie and Port Seton had the distinct advantage in the early part of the twentieth century of being connected to Edinburgh via a tram line. It was initiated as an extension of the Musselburgh Electric Light and Traction Company's Levenhall to Joppa line. The development of the line was problematic as it involved protracted negotiations between landowners, local authorities and the company's representatives, most of whom came from the parent organisation in London. Once the line was opened it provided the most convenient means of getting to work for many of the colliers who worked in the coastal pits. Most of the colliery housing was clustered in groups close to the tramway at Cockenzie, Prestonpans, the Cuthill, Morison's Haven and so into Levenhall and Musselburgh.

The contiguous villages of Cockenzie and Port Seton border a rocky stretch of coastline between their respective harbours. A small bay in the centre of this stretch served as a convenient place for beaching fishing craft and was probably the first port on this part of the coast. Many of the villages' houses extended right onto the rocks above the foreshore. Several of them had once been used as salt works – over twenty such were in operation during the eighteenth century, producing salt from sea water. Natural seaside rockponds were enlarged or improved with dams. From these sea water was laded by 'bucket and wand' or force pumps into the coal-fired cast iron pans. Salt was raked from the pans and dried in a 'girnel' or barn. As salt was highly taxed all these operations were under the supervision of excisemen. Several local tales recount the (often successful) attempts of the salters to deceive their watchers and spirit away some of the salt untaxed.

Cockenzie Harbour was extensively refurbished for the Cadell family, who spent £6,000 on the port to support their shipping business. The work was carried out by Robert Stevenson in the 1830s. The Cadells' main interests were once in the estate of Tranent and its coal mines, but they invested the revenues from this source in overseas trading ventures, salt pans and other industrial concerns at sites along the coast near Cockenzie. The harbour was quickly adopted by local fishermen and boat-building has long been carried out at the harbour's edge.

PORT SETON, HARBOUR. 1182

Port Seton Harbour was once the property of the Earls of Winton, but the family lost their lands to the York Building Company (an early example of a London-based investment company) after supporting the wrong side in the Jacobite uprising of 1715. The company developed the harbour as a coal port, along with that of Cockenzie (where they installed Scotland's first railway, with wooden rails running from their pits at Tranent to the harbour side). The fishermen of Port Seton were regarded as adventurous – many fished 30 miles offshore in open cobles (far beyond where fishermen from other nearby harbours were prepared to go). In the nineteenth century it was common to spend a period signed up on whaling expeditions to Greenland and later, in the twentieth century, to the Antarctic. There is still a substantial community involved in the fishing industry, but the local boats are often based at other ports for considerable periods.

Port Seton Harbour is less than a kilometre from the harbour at Cockenzie. It was rebuilt in its current form as a result of an initiative by local fishermen in the Victorian period who needed a safer anchorage than the existing ruinous harbour, which had suffered from a lack of investment since the failure of the York Building Company, the one-time owners. Supported by the Earl of Wemyss, the main landowner in the area at the time, funds were raised to pay the firm of D. & T. Stevenson to carry out the work in 1880. The harbour was given an inner and outer basin, and at one time over eighty large fishing boats operated from the port.

88708 PORT SETON FROM THE HARBOUR

The Boat Shore was used as Cockenzie and Port Seton's open-air fish market in the nineteenth and early twentieth centuries. Catches were laid out on the rocks and sold to the highest bidder, an affair that always drew spectators to see the show. Some had a professional interest – such as the merchants and cadgers who might need to know prices prior to making their own bids – but others were there purely for entertainment.

This picture captures the bustle at the Boat Shore fish market. Selling the catch was left to the fishermen's womenfolk, who tended to control the family finances. All along the coast fishwives were renowned for their independence and acumen, at a time when these traits were generally not attributed to women. Fishwives wore a distinctive costume consisting of a printed cotton blouse and full skirt with an apron or overskirt that could be gathered up. A shawl completed the ensemble. The open space of the Boat Shore had many other uses including drying washing, mending boats and nets, and laying sails and equipment out to dry.

MAIN STREET, ABERLADY.

Aberlady gained a reputation as a pleasant place for a summer holiday amongst the more retiring Victorian and Edwardian visitors to East Lothian. The charms of the coast could be enjoyed to best advantage but without experiencing the distractions of nearby Gullane and North Berwick. All the same, both places were only a short journey away for a day trip. Most of the accommodation in Aberlady was comprised of ordinary homes and cottages leased by the week, month or quarter, and offered with or without attendance. In the former case, the proprietor (or a servant) prepared meals and kept house for the lessee.

Aberlady Cross signals the village's ancient right to hold markets and fairs. It lies on the north side of the main street and has lost its top – only the pillar shaft remains. The street is lined with a mixture of single-storey cottages and more substantial dwellings. The main activity of today's visitors is golf: Kilspindie golf course lies between the village and the sea; the links courses of Gullane and Luffness are just to the west. In the distant past, Aberlady was associated with the development of Christianity in the Lothians. There was a community of Culdees (Celtic monks) here in antiquity and a replica of an eighth century Anglian cross-shaft, which was found nearby, is kept in Aberlady church: the original is preserved in the collections of the National Museums of Scotland.

Aberlady's position on the coast at the mouth of the Peffer Burn was exploited by the burgesses of Haddington who secured the village as their port. In medieval times the bay was much deeper than it is today, and ships trading with Haddington merchants were able to approach very close to the present village. However, silting and the growth of sandbanks and mudflats rendered it useless as a port. The last regular users have been captured in this photograph, which shows a string of herring boats beached on the sands, a safe lie-up over the winter. The boats were some of the hundreds that followed the shoals of herring from the north of Scotland to the south of England as they migrated down the North Sea.

Luffness Mill lies between Aberlady and Gullane on the Peffer Burn and is typical of the small country mills that once dotted the East Lothian landscape. It has been disused for many years, but serves as a reminder of the time when farmers were tied ('thirled', in old Scots terminology) to a local mill. This practice was universal, and almost universally hated, because the obligation could not be avoided and a corrupt miller could easily manipulate the system to enrich himself by giving false weight while still being guaranteed a steady supply of custom. In East Lothian, country mills were so widespread that any source of running water – even a slow-moving stream such as the Peffer – was pressed into service. Only a few survived into the twentieth century, and in East Lothian only Prestonmill near East Linton remains in working condition, under the supervision of the National Trust for Scotland.

Gullane beach was discovered by Edinburgh families in the nineteenth century and its subsequent popularity led to the entire face of the village changing. Gullane even gained a railway station served by a spur from the North British Railway's main line – in the first part of the twentieth century summer specials brought thousands of trippers for a day at the sands. Most of those who occupied the villas and hotels in Gullane took the precaution of securing a beach hut (of which there were many) for the duration of their stay. These provided a secure base on the busy beach and a convenient shelter if the weather was uncertain.

Gullane is nearly surrounded by rolling sand dunes that have at times almost overwhelmed the village. It was almost abandoned in the seventeenth century, but recovered in the eighteenth century to become Scotland's foremost centre for training racehorses, the well-drained ground being ideal for the purpose. The training grounds were also well adapted to another purpose, and today are covered with a series of golf courses, probably the best group of natural links courses in Scotland. The dunes can only really be seen on the north side of the village, as in this photograph, and provide a multitude of pathways to a wide sandy beach. In the last forty years pioneering efforts to stabilise the dunes have included planting windbreaks and restoring vegetation. The whole area had been placed in great danger of erosion from crowds of holidaymakers using the beach.

Gullane prospered on the back of the Victorians' enthusiasm for healthy, restorative holidays by the seaside and made a remarkable recovery from its position of virtual abandonment in the seventeenth century. By the dawn of the twentieth century new streets had been laid out for rows of villas and large detached houses, most of which were rented out to visitors during the summer months. In the centre of the village a full complement of shops was developed, tradesmen became established, and several hotels, restaurants and tea-rooms were opened.

Bisset's Hotel, Gullane.

Bisset's Hotel had a prominent site on Gullane's main street, and its imposing façade was an obvious sign of the prosperity of the village a hundred years ago. It was built in 1894 for James Bisset who had been a butler at nearby Archerfield House (this was a common career move at the time). Bisset's was only one of several similar hotels that together could cater for several hundred residents. The Golf Inn was just across the road, and there was also the Lodge (which became the Queens Hotel), while the Marine Hotel, now the centrepiece of the Scottish Fire Services Training School, was situated on the eastern outskirts of the village.

Gullane smithy was in the centre of the village. In the early 1900s it was a picturesque relic of an earlier time when the village was a centre for the neighbouring farms and not a holiday resort. However, it was still a functioning workshop and probably even busier than ever. As large houses were built every year to accommodate the tourists who flocked to Gullane, one of the smith's tasks would have been to make fences and gates for new developments nearby. Horses still had to be shod and carriages brought by visitors or rented from locals needed their wheels repaired or fitted with fresh tyres. Even the mundane tasks of the kitchen, such as knife-sharpening, might be taken care of: there is a large round sharpening stone positioned against the wall behind the sitting boy.

Dirleton is one of the most delightful of East Lothian's villages. The oldest houses are set around an extensive green, one side of which is occupied by the remains of a medieval castle and its grounds, now a Historic Scotland property. This photograph was taken from the castle walls and shows the recreated formal garden. An old story runs that Dirleton was only a tiny community until nearby Gullane, the main village in the parish, began to be swallowed up by drifting sand in the seventeenth century. The villagers of Gullane were forced to abandon their homes and Dirleton was feued out (divided into plots with a secure tenure) on a regular plan to accommodate the displaced population.

The ruins of Dirleton Castle still manage to suggest its strength. It was once a place of power, serving as the headquarters of a local baron. The castle sits on a rocky outcrop and is compactly constructed with a series of towers and a curtain wall. The site was improved by excavating a ditch, part of which still survives beneath the gateway. The earliest parts of the castle date from the time of John de Vaux, who was seneschal (the chief household officer) to Alexander II's queen. The castle was extended by the Halyburton family who secured the Barony of Dirleton in the fourteenth century, and also by the Ruthvens who succeeded them in the sixteenth century; surviving features of the ruins can be traced to the time of both these families. It was once described as the most desirable stronghold in Scotland, but it suffered when its garrison attempted to stand up to Cromwell's troops, who left it in a ruinous condition after taking it in 1650.

The interior of Dirleton Castle was left in a terrible condition by Cromwell's troops, when they despoiled the castle in the 1650s. No longer habitable or desirable as a residence, it was left to nature for several centuries and became quite overgrown, as this picture reveals. There is little in this view to suggest the attraction that the castle held for Logan of Restalrig, who coveted it so much that he was prepared to plot against James VI to secure it. The castle and lands of Dirleton instead went to Sir Thomas Erskine who saved the king from the plotters. Today the ivy has been stripped away to reveal the remains of the interior ranges and domestic fittings, as well as a prison located under the castle chapel.

Like the other coastal villages, Dirleton was popular in summer with holiday visitors. Many of the houses in its East End were taken on long-term lease by families taking a summer-long break. Although the village provided little in the way of entertainment, the bright lights of North Berwick lay just to the east and the wide sporting grounds of Gullane Links were only a short journey to the west. The coast nearby was popular for picnics, when children might be spellbound with tales of the smugglers and wreckers who once haunted the coast. If the East End of Dirleton was popular with holidaymakers, the West End was perhaps more prosaic, as this row of cottages reveals. Most of the village's inhabitants were once workers on nearby farms. There were eighteen farms in the parish that, until recent times, demanded a considerable manpower. In addition there were freestone quarries, brick and tile works (one at the wonderfully named 'Pudden Butts') and a maltings at Fenton.

Whitekirk Parish Church. Destroyed by Fire. 26/2/14.   No. 2.   Photo by C. Bruce Haddington.

This photograph of Whitekirk Church was taken by Charles Bruce of Haddington the morning after a fire destroyed much of the interior. It was quickly discovered that the fire had been started by the militant wing of the Edwardian Women's Suffrage Movement: it was an emphatic sign that the movement was active in East Lothian. Quite why St Mary's was selected for their action is still a mystery, despite national and local police (and press) investigations at the time, as the church was in a quiet location and well off the beaten track. The church is near the site of a medieval holy well, a place of miracles on the pilgrim route to St Andrews. At one time thousands stopped to take the water every year; today an annual ecumenical walk from Haddington to Whitekirk commemorates the early pilgrims.

Whitekirk.

Whitekirk is another 'secret village', as its only street is hidden from the main road to North Berwick, which bends sharply away at the church. To the west of the church the street rises as it skirts Whitekirk Hill and the houses peter out leaving a narrow road winding between fields. The street is lined with single-storey cottages, although there are a few more substantial dwellings at the southern end. Once, the population was predominantly composed of agricultural workers who served on the many nearby farms, along with the skilled craftsmen necessary to maintain the farms' equipment in good working order. Whitekirk Farm itself fetched a very high rental – it had a good mix of arable and grazing land, once reserved for a prize herd of Leicester sheep.

Tyninghame is one of the prettiest of the East Lothian villages, with gardens in front of and behind the houses, which are set well back from the road. Once again, this is an artificial layout designed to accommodate the wishes of a landscaping proprietor (the Earl of Haddington) at the end of the eighteenth century. As the original settlement was in the way of his new parkland around Tyninghame House, it had to move. Luckily, the new village was very carefully planned and served well as the pattern for an estate village. Most of the buildings standing today date from the middle of the nineteenth century. The rows of estate workers' cottages are interspersed with more substantial properties, among them the well-designed old schoolhouse, baker's house, smith's house and post office.

TYNNINGHAME VILLAGE.

As a planned village, Tyninghame was provided with all the facilities needed to ensure the smooth running of the estate. By the time it was being laid out the ideas initiated by East Lothian's proprietors in the eighteenth century had had time to develop and, with the benefit of this experience, a well-balanced community was planned. A property was provided for the estate factor (the general manager) and others for craftsmen and small shopkeepers. The sawmill in this picture, positioned beside the River Tyne, was built in 1828 and provided with a waterwheel and other fittings from George Sked's foundry in Dunbar. It was used to prepare timber from the Earl of Haddington's extensive woodlands.

Despite appearances to the contrary today, West Barns was once an industrial village. At the end of the nineteenth and beginning of the twentieth centuries three large factories and a number of smaller ones together employed several hundred hands. Seafield Brick and Tile Works lay on the village's eastern flank with Annandale's Paper Works to the west; both gained a reputation for innovation and productivity. The white-harled building in the centre of this photograph was part of a maltings and distillery complex. This was built on the site of Dunbar's old town mills and was supplied with water by a mill lade (which is still there even though the buildings have been taken down). The village hall on the right was built as a reading room in 1901.

West Barns and Hedderwick Links were often used by the local Yeomanry regiment for summer exercises and camps. This photograph was taken in 1912 when the old East Lothian Yeomanry Cavalry had been forced to abandon its Victorian traditions and uniforms and had been integrated into the Territorial Army as the Lothians and Border Horse. Their role on mobilisation was intended to be as the forward troops and scouts for a division of infantry. Their training reflected this with manoeuvres at troop and squadron strength in the nearby countryside, sometimes to the consternation of the locals. At least once a section of Yeomanry was caught dressed as holidaymakers (both male and female) as they tried to infiltrate a line of pickets during a war game.

Musical Ride Coy.
Lothians & Berwickshire Imp. Yeo.

During the Victorian heyday of the Yeomanry, when they were very much regarded as East Lothian's county regiment, the annual camp at Hedderwick was one of the events of the season. Balls and dinners were a regular part of the summer fortnight and at the completion of their compulsory training the regiment held a very competitive series of horse races on a course laid out on the links (the prizes were as much as 100 guineas, well over what a working man could expect to earn annually). Entertainment was always provided by the regiment's mounted band and their elite Musical Ride Company (above), who led their mounts through intricate patterns at the trot and gallop.

Duke Street, Belhaven, DUNBAR

"Bisset Series"

Belhaven had the same relationship with Dunbar as Aberlady had with Haddington: it was the town's medieval port. Ships were beached on Belhaven Sands and goods loaded to and from carts drawn up alongside at low tide. Nowadays, there are no signs of the landing places and the village is a cluster of several small streets at the western perimeter of Dunbar. Their position away from the main road gives them a character all of their own, which maintains the air of time bygone. Hidden amongst the ordinary cottages are a few gems: the building on the left is a very old (and small-scale) L-shaped house with a tower stair in the inner angle.

Belhaven Brewery has grown to be one of East Lothian's success stories in recent times. Its origins date to the eighteenth century, although there is an even older tradition of monastic brewing on the site. Patrick Dunbar, Earl of March, granted the monks of the May Island a 'toft' or piece of land here in the twelfth century and their spring still exists today on the site of the present brewery. For much of its history the brewery was in the hands of the Dudgeon family and its sales were strictly local; the main part of the business was concerned with malting barley of which there was an abundant supply from nearby farms. However, in the 1960s the firm went public and despite some uncertain times has entered the twenty-first century as a national brand. Now a fleet of giant lorries transports its keg and bottled beers the length and breadth of Britain, and the brand is making good progress in international markets.

Belhaven lies on what was the Great North Road at its approach to Dunbar, which is just a measured mile away (the exact distance between Belhaven and Dunbar post offices). In this photograph, a coach heading for the town has paused for the photographer adjacent to Archibald Kerr's house and grocery warehouse (the building behind the tree on the right). Kerr himself is in the photograph – he is the man wearing the white apron. The house was built by his father, who took over an existing grocery and redeveloped the site in the 1850s. Most of the other buildings in the picture date from the same period.

This photograph was taken at the corner of Brewery Lane in Belhaven and captures a band of village characters taking their ease in a sunny spot. Most of them lived nearby – for example William Kirkwood, on the extreme right, lived at 12 High Street, which was only a few steps away. The window behind them belonged to one of Belhaven's small groceries. Over the years all of the local shops have closed, and Belhaven's residents have to shop at Dunbar or travel even further afield.

By the time this photograph was taken in the early twentieth century, Broxburn had declined to little more than a hamlet made up of a group of cottages by the roadside on the south-east of Dunbar. Up until the middle of the previous century it had been able to offer several tradesmen employment and had a considerably larger population, with well over 150 people living in the immediate locality. Its smithy – and later a large garage – were the last surviving trading premises. The houses on the left were built for workers on nearby farms, but by the time they had been constructed employment opportunities in farming were strictly limited. Nearby Dunbar pulled in many of the households that once made their home in Broxburn because there were more jobs available in the town.

Thornton Sands were important to Innerwick for two reasons. Firstly, they drew their fair share of holiday visitors and excursionists, so boosting the local economy. Secondly and probably more importantly, they provided farmers with a steady supply of seaweed that, properly rotted, formed an excellent fertiliser. This practice was remarked upon by Sir William Brereton (an English traveller) in 1636, and by the nineteenth century farmers were able to keep their coastal fields continually under grain, abandoning the usual procedure of crop rotation practised elsewhere to preserve and maximise fertility. As long as the fields had an annual dressing of seaware the harvest was high and the grain commanded high prices at Dunbar and Haddington Corn Exchanges.

THORNTON LOCH SANDS, NEAR COCKBURNSPATH.

Thorntonloch is the second village in Innerwick parish, and was once home to a substantial community of fishermen and agricultural labourers, plus a few tradesmen and lime burners. There were even some salt pans there. The village lies on the coast below the Thornton Glen and had a small harbour for importing coal and exporting lime. Towards the end of the nineteenth century and well into the twentieth, Thorntonloch was a popular place for summer excursions and picnics as this photograph shows. Special trains could discharge their passengers at nearby Innerwick station, or convoys of charabancs (large open-topped buses) could be organised for a run down from Dunbar.

THORNTON LOCH, INNERWICK

SKATERAW LIFEBOAT, DUNBAR.

Skateraw Bay was the site chosen to keep the Dunbar No. 2 Lifeboat in 1907. The boathouse was placed just above the tide line and a concrete ramp was built to run the boat carriage beyond the surf to launch the boat. For the entire history of the station, William Runciman Fairbairn was the coxswain of this lifeboat, the *Sarah Kay*, as well as serving as coxswain of successive Dunbar boats. His service is still unparalleled in East Lothian's RNLI history. The lifeboat was stationed here to increase the launch options available to the Dunbar crew. Dunbar Harbour was sometimes stormbound and on occasion its lifeboat had to be hauled by road to Skateraw. With a boat on site, only the crew needed to muster at the bay thus saving valuable time in rescues.